9/96

OUR LIVING WORLD

Patterns in Nature:
An Overview of the Living World

By **Jenny Tesar**

Series Editor: Vincent Marteka
Introduction by John Behler, *New York Zoological Society*

A BLACKBIRCH PRESS BOOK
WOODBRIDGE, CONNECTICUT

Published by Blackbirch Press, Inc.
260 Amity Rd.
Woodbridge, CT 06525

Printed in Canada

10 9 8 7 6 5 4 3 2

Editorial Director: Bruce Glassman
Editor: Tanya Lee Stone
Assistant Editor: Elizabeth M. Taylor
Design Director: Sonja Kalter
Production: Sandra Burr, Rudy Raccio, Madeline Parker

Library of Congress Cataloging-in-Publication Data

Tesar, Jenny E.
    Patterns in nature: an overview of the living world / by Jenny Tesar.—1st ed.
        p.   cm.
    Includes bibliographical references and index.
    ISBN 1-56711-058-4
    1. Biology—Juvenile literature. [1. Biology.] I. Title.
QH309.2.T47   1994
574—dc20   93-50748
                                                         CIP
                                                         AC

Contents

What Does It Mean to Be "Alive"?

Introduction by John Behler,
New York Zoological Society

One summer morning, as I was walking through a beautiful field, I was inspired to think about what it really means to be "alive." Part of the answer, I came to realize, was right in front of my eyes.

The meadow was ablaze with color, packed with wildflowers at the height of their blooming season. A multitude of insects, warmed by the sun's early-morning rays, began to stir. Painted turtles sunned themselves on an old mossy log in a nearby pond. A pair of wood ducks whistled a call as they flew overhead, resting near a shagbark hickory on the other side of the pond.

As I wandered through this unspoiled habitat, I paused at a patch of milkweed to look for monarch-butterfly caterpillars, which depend on the milkweed's leaves for food. Indeed, the caterpillars were there, munching away. Soon these larvae would spin their cocoons, emerge as beautiful orange-and-black butterflies, and begin a fantastic 1,500-mile (2,400-kilometer) migration to wintering grounds in Mexico. It took biologists nearly one hundred years to unravel the life history of these butterflies. Watching them in the milkweed patch made me wonder how much more there is to know about these insects and all the other living organisms in just that one meadow.

The patterns of the natural world have often been likened to a spider's web, and for good reason. All life on Earth is interconnected in an elegant yet surprisingly simple design, and each living thing is an essential part of that design. To understand biology and the functions of living things, biologists have spent a lot of time looking at the differences among organisms. But in order to understand the very nature of living things, we must first understand what they have in common.

The butterfly larvae and the milkweed—and all animals and plants, for that matter—are made up of the same basic elements. These elements are obtained, used, and eliminated by every living thing in a series of chemical activities called metabolism.

Every molecule of every living tissue must contain carbon. During photosynthesis, green plants take in carbon dioxide from the atmosphere. Within their chlorophyll-filled leaves, in the presence of sunlight, the carbon dioxide is combined with water to form sugar—nature's most basic food. Animals need carbon, too. To grow and function, animals must eat plants or other animals that have fed on plants in order to obtain carbon. When plants and animals die, bacteria and fungi help to break down their tissues. This allows the carbon in plants and animals to be recycled. Indeed, the carbon in your body—and everyone else's body—may once have been inside a dinosaur, a giant redwood, or a monarch butterfly!

All life also needs nitrogen. Nitrogen is an essential component of protoplasm, the complex of chemicals that makes up living cells. Animals acquire nitrogen in the same manner as they acquire carbon dioxide: by eating plants or other animals that have eaten plants. Plants, however, must rely on nitrogen-fixing bacteria in the soil to absorb nitrogen from the atmosphere and convert it into proteins. These proteins are then absorbed from the soil by plant roots.

Living things start life as a single cell. The process by which cells grow and reproduce to become a specific organism—whether the organism is an oak tree or a whale—is controlled by two basic substances called deoxyribonucleic acid (DNA) and ribonucleic acid (RNA). These two chemicals are the building blocks of genes that determine how an organism looks, grows, and functions. Each organism has a unique pattern of DNA and RNA in its genes. This pattern determines all the characteristics of a living thing. Each species passes its unique pattern from generation to generation. Over many billions of years, a process involving genetic mutation and natural selection has allowed species to adapt to a constantly changing environment by evolving—changing genetic patterns. The living creatures we know today are the results of these adaptations.

Reproduction and growth are important to every species, since these are the processes by which new members of a species are created. If a species cannot reproduce and adapt, or if it cannot reproduce fast enough to replace those members that die, it will become extinct (no longer exist).

In recent years, biologists have learned a great deal about how living things function. But there is still much to learn about nature. With high-technology equipment and new information, exciting discoveries are being made every day. New insights and theories quickly make many biology textbooks obsolete. One thing, however, will forever remain certain: As living things, we share an amazing number of characteristics with other forms of life. As animals, our survival depends upon the food and functions provided by other animals and plants. As humans—who can understand the similarities and interdependence among living things—we cannot help but feel connected to the natural world, and we cannot forget our responsibility to protect it. It is only through looking at, and understanding, the rest of the natural world that we can truly appreciate what it means to be "alive."

1

The Amazing Variety of Living Things

 High on a mountain, a goat leaps from rock to rock. In a puddle formed by rainwater, tiny one-celled organisms chase one another. On icy Antarctica, penguins gather to raise their young. Deep in the ocean, where sunlight never reaches, a fish with built-in lights hunts for food. In a tropical rainforest, a bat feeds on ripe figs.

Everywhere on the Earth there is life: on land, in water, and in the air. Each kind of environment, or habitat, has its own community of living things. Grasslands are home to grasses, wildflowers, rabbits, and hawks. Rocky beaches are home to starfish, crabs, barnacles, and seaweeds. Sandy deserts are home to cacti, lizards, and kangaroo rats. Each organism is adapted to life in its environment. Starfish and seaweeds are adapted to life in ocean water. Cacti and kangaroo rats are adapted to life in a very

Opposite:
Living things come in an infinite variety of shapes and sizes. Even the world of these microscopic creatures is filled with thousands of beautiful, intricately patterned organisms.

dry environment. Move a starfish to a desert, or a cactus to an ocean, and each will quickly die.

Scientists have identified about 1.5 million different kinds, or species, of living things. A species is a group of organisms that shares more traits with one another than with other organisms and that can reproduce with one another. House cats are a species. White pines are a species. Humans are a species.

The smallest known organisms are a species of bacteria so tiny that a row of 25,000 of them would equal only 1 inch (2.5 centimeters). The largest animal is the blue whale. A blue whale may be 100 feet (30 meters) long and weigh 260,000 pounds (118,000 kilograms). Even larger than blue whales are the sequoia trees of California. A mature sequoia may grow to a height of more than 300 feet (91 meters)

The largest animal ever to inhabit the Earth is the blue whale, which can grow to a length of 100 feet (30 meters) and can weigh 260,000 pounds (118,000 kilograms).

and can weigh up to 1,000 tons (2 million pounds, or 907 metric tons).

Each species is unique—different from every other species. Sometimes the differences seem very slight. The black mountain salamander and the seal salamander look very similar. Both are chubby, brown salamanders with long tails. Both live in damp mountain habitats in the eastern United States. But the two salamanders have different markings, and the black mountain salamander lives in water, whereas the seal salamander spends most of its time on land.

In other cases, of course, it is very easy to tell species apart. It is easy to see that cats, pine trees, and humans are different species. And yet, no matter how great the differences among all these organisms, all share certain similarities.

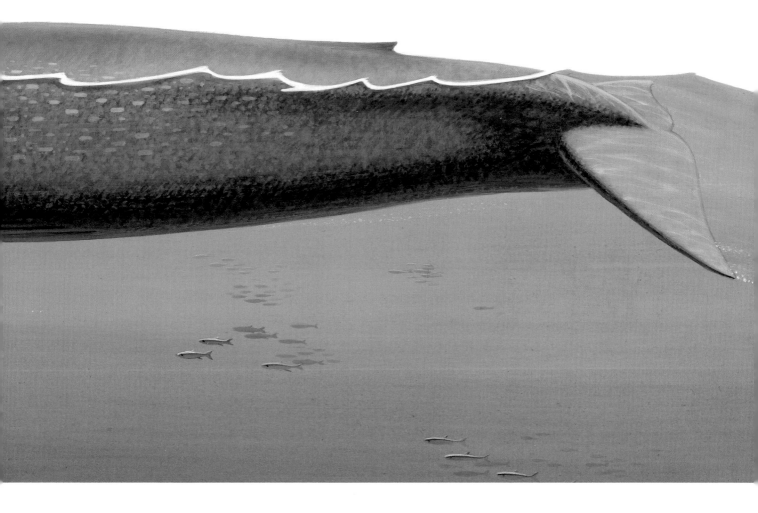

Anatomy of a Cell

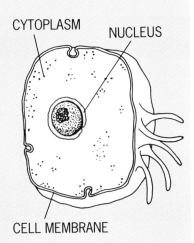

CYTOPLASM   NUCLEUS

CELL MEMBRANE

All living things are made up of a varying number of cells. A bacterium such as this one is made up of only one cell. A more complex organism, such as a cat or a rosebush, is made up of billions of cells.

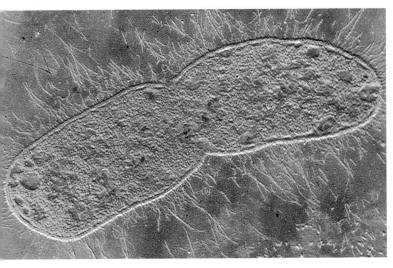

What Is Life?

Moss grows on a rock. Sharks swim through water. Bedbugs make someone's mattress their home. How does moss differ from a rock? How are sharks different from water? How are bedbugs different from a mattress?

Moss, sharks, bedbugs, and all other living things have four basic characteristics:

Response They react to changes in their environment, including attacks by enemies and changes in the amount of moisture or sunlight.

Metabolism They use food to produce energy, which is needed for movement, respiration, and all other life activities.

Reproduction They create more individuals of the same kind. For example, moss produces new moss plants and sharks produce new sharks.

Growth They pass through a life cycle that includes birth, growth, and eventually death.

Building Blocks Called Cells

Another similarity among living things is that they are all made of small units called cells. Some organisms are made of a single cell—bacteria and protozoans are one-celled organisms. Other organisms, such as humans and corn plants, are made of billions of cells.

Cells come in many different shapes and sizes, though most are so small that they can be seen only through a microscope. But the basic structure and operation of almost all cells are similar, with the same three main parts: the membrane, the nucleus, and the cytoplasm.

A Chimpanzee Is Like You and Me

Human

As scientists have studied the daily lives of chimpanzees, they have discovered many similarities between these apes and humans. Like humans, chimpanzees use tools. They use stones as hammers to open hard-shelled nuts. They use twigs to remove nuts from cracked shells and insects from nests. They even use leaves to scoop up water and to wipe dirt off their bodies.

Chimpanzees live and work in groups, just like humans do. Several members of a chimpanzee community will work together to surround and kill prey. Then these hunters will share the meat with other members of their group.

Humans have larger brains than chimpanzees and are more intelligent. But the chimpanzee brain is very similar to that of a human. It is obvious that chimpanzees can think, learn, and remember things. For example, they remember where they leave their stone hammers.

Chimpanzees show joy, fear, sadness, and many other emotions seen in humans. Their gestures are similar to ours, too. They even kiss and hold hands!

Chimpanzee

The cell membrane is the skin of the cell; it protects the cell's insides and gives the cell its form. The nucleus is a small round structure that is the control center of the cell, regulating all the cell's activities. The cytoplasm includes everything that is between the nucleus and the cell membrane; it is the machinery of the cell, where energy is produced and new cell parts are built.

Genes Within the nucleus are structures called genes. Genes determine the traits, or characteristics, of the cell and of the entire organism. They are the units of heredity. Genes determine whether a cell will be a bone cell or a muscle cell, whether an organism is a bird or a whale, and whether it is a male or a female.

Organisms that are closely related have very similar genetic material. For example, chimpanzees are the closest living relatives of humans. More than 98 percent of the genetic material in chimpanzees and humans is the same! This explains why there are so many similarities, both in structure and behavior, between the two species.

DID YOU KNOW

Monkey Business

Chimpanzees are the closest living relatives to humans. In fact, the two species share more than 98 percent of their genetic material.

Color plays an important role in the lives of both plants and animals. Certain plants rely on their bright colors to attract insects that will help in pollination, which is part of the plant's reproductive process.

Surprising Similarities

To survive, all living things must find solutions to common problems: how to obtain food, how to avoid enemies, and how to make sure their young survive. Sometimes, organisms have very different solutions to these problems. In other cases, however, their solutions are strikingly similar.

Many plants depend on bright colors to attract insects, which play an important role in the plants' reproduction. For example, zinnia plants have bright yellow or red flowers, which attract bees. Many animals also depend on bright colors as part of their

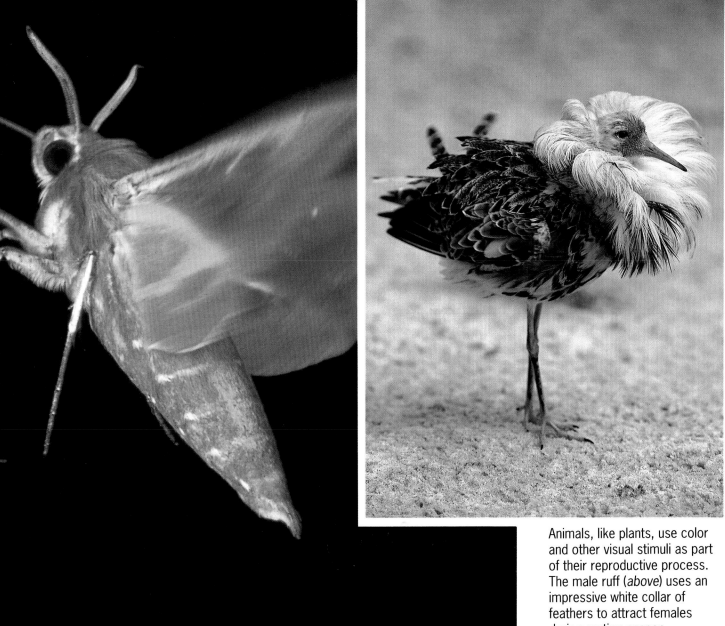

Animals, like plants, use color and other visual stimuli as part of their reproductive process. The male ruff (*above*) uses an impressive white collar of feathers to attract females during mating season.

reproductive process. These animals use dramatic displays of colors and other physical features to attract mates so that they can reproduce. For example, male American goldfinches have bright yellow feathers, which attract female goldfinches.

Plants and animals share similar protective adaptations for their young. The seeds of most plants are surrounded by hard coats. Similarly, the eggs of many animals are surrounded by hard shells. These hard outer coverings protect the developing plants and animals against enemies, against accidental damage, and against drying.

Humans and other mammal young are protected inside their mothers' bodies until birth. Once they are born, they are given great care for a relatively long period of time, compared to other animals. When a human mother wants to go shopping, she can take her baby along. She can carry the baby on her back or in a sling across her front. Many other animals also carry their infants from place to place. At first, a baboon mother carries her baby across her front; when the baby is older, it travels on the mother's back. Newborn wolf spiders also cling to their mother's back for their first week of life. This provides them with protection they need to best ensure their survival. A cat uses her teeth to hold a kitten by loose skin on the back of the kitten's neck as it is carried from place to place. A sea otter carries her infant on her belly as she floats in the ocean. As a mother bat flies through the sky, her baby uses its teeth to hang onto her fur. As a grebe swims— and even dives under the water—her chick holds onto the feathers on her back.

The male anole lizard relies on his bright red throat sac to get the attention of his possible mates.

Past, Present, and Future

No one knows for sure when life began on Earth, or exactly how it started. Scientists continue to debate this issue, every year developing new ideas and hypotheses about the very origins of existence. For example, researchers believed for a long time that life evolved very gradually—over a long period of time—in a calm environment billions of years ago. New research, however, indicates that the beginnings of life were neither leisurely nor under calm conditions. New theories propose that life began on a planet that was constantly bombarded by meteor explosions and volcanic eruptions—in a quick, heated, and violent manner.

Protection of young is one behavior that many animals have in common. The female wolf spider (*above*) carries her newborns on her back for about a week before they jump off to be on their own. Like other marsupials, these baby opossums (*below*) cling to their mother inside a pouch for protection as they develop.

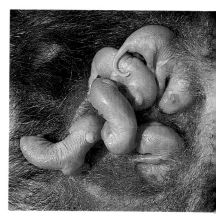

The earliest known forms of life lived in water about 3.5 billion years ago. They were very simple forms of bacteria. As millions upon millions of years passed, more complex living things appeared in the Earth's waters, including algae, sponges, and jellyfish. Eventually, even larger organisms appeared, and organisms moved into all the different habitats on Earth.

By the time the first humans appeared on Earth, the seas had long been filled with fish, whales, and sea turtles. The land was home to thousands of species of trees, grasses, insects, birds, snakes, monkeys, and numerous other creatures.

Fossils tell us about life of long ago. Fossils are remains, or traces, of living things that have been preserved in rocks, ice, and other materials. Fossils tell us of the many fabulous creatures that once lived on Earth, such as strange worm-like animals, giant tree ferns, and fierce dinosaurs.

Members of the Human Family

DRYOPITHICUS

First appeared about
12 million years ago

Ancient primate widely
thought to be direct
ancestor of living
African apes.

RAMAPITHICUS

About 14 million years
ago

Thought by many to
be the first hominid,
but its classification
is disputed—some
scientists believe it
was still a member
of the ape family.

AUSTRALOPITHICUS

More than 4 million
years ago

Very early member of
the human family.
Walked upright and
had a larger brain than
average ape species.
Often classified in
between an ape and
the first human
species, *Homo habilis.*

Fossils provide evidence that life has gradually changed with time. This gradual change in organisms is known as evolution. Other evidence for evolution includes similarities in genes, structure, and development.

Humans are part of this evolution. About 5 million years ago, some apes began to develop in ways that led to chimpanzees and a variety of ape species that exist today. Other apes began to develop in ways

HOMO HABILIS	HOMO ERECTUS	NEANDERTHAL HUMAN	CRO-MAGNON HUMAN	MODERN HUMAN
About 1.9 million years ago	About 1.6 million years ago	More than 100,000 years ago	100,000 years ago	About 40,000 years ago
Less robust jaw than australopithicus, smaller teeth, and a larger brain. Used primitive stone tools.	Limbs and skeleton much thicker than that of modern humans but very similar in bodily structure and proportion.	Shorter than modern human, longer skull, lower forehead, but a comparable brain size.	Shorter and broader face than Neanderthal, reduced brow ridge, and reduced incisor and canine teeth.	High brow, large brain cavity, lightest skeletal frame.

that led to humans. Millions of years passed before the evolution to humans was complete.

Living things are still changing, or evolving. Some species are developing ways to adapt to changing environmental conditions. Other species are having difficulty adapting to their changing environment. These species are in danger of dying out, or becoming extinct. If this happens, they will be gone forever, just like the giant tree ferns and the fierce dinosaurs.

The Amazing Variety of Living Things

2

Responding to Changes in the Environment

 Someone calls your name...and you look up. A breeze blows...and a holly tree's leaves clump together. A mouse leaves a trail of scent...and a snake follows the trail. Sunlight hits a pond...and small fish swim into the shadows.

The environment of every organism is constantly changing. Some changes are not important to the organism. Other changes can be deadly. To survive, the organism must be aware of changes in its environment, and it must be able to respond to these changes.

Any change in the environment that is detected by an organism is called a stimulus. An organism's response to a stimulus is called a reaction. When a friend calls your name, that is a stimulus. Your reaction is to look at the friend. The scent of a mouse is a stimulus for a snake. The snake reacts by going after the scent, hoping to find and eat the mouse.

Opposite:
All living things must respond effectively to changes in the environment in order to survive. Chameleons have a number of unique adaptations that enable them to react to stimuli, including two eyes that can move independently in different directions and an ability to change color in order to match their surroundings.

Venus's-Flytrap: A Big Surprise for Flies

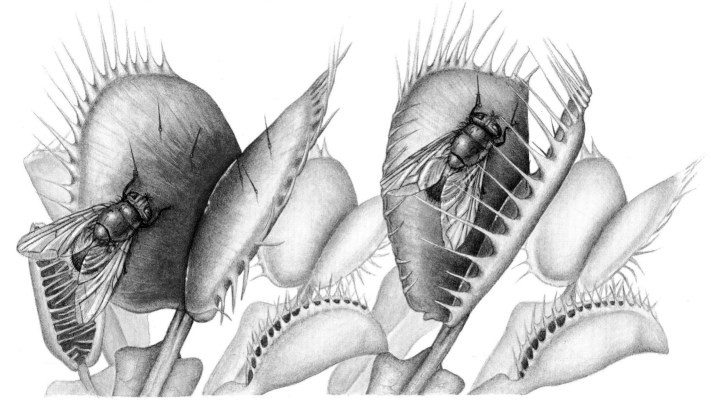

A fly lands on the plant, touching the sensitive hairs.

Chemical reactions in the hairs send electrical signals to the hinge, telling it to close.

Organisms detect stimuli in different ways. Green plants and fungi seem to receive stimuli through certain cells, such as those at the tips of growing parts. Most animals have special sense organs, such as eyes and ears, that detect stimuli.

Plant Reactions

Plants seem so still. In fact, they are in constant motion. Stems twist and turn, leaves bend and curl, flowers open and close. These movements are the reactions to changes in the plants' environment.

Some important plant stimuli include light, temperature, water, gravity, touch, chemicals, and wind. If the stimulus is useful, the plant usually moves toward it. If the stimulus is harmful, the plant will usually move away from it.

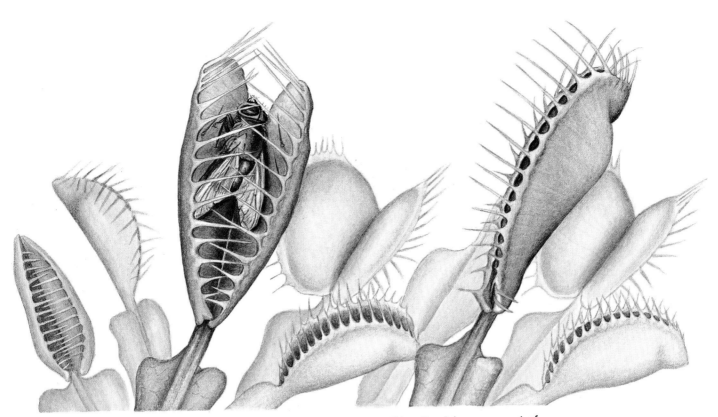

In an instant, the fly is trapped inside the plant.

Digestive juices pour out of the leaf and begin to break down the insect's body. The leaf will reopen in 7 to 10 days.

The stem of a plant usually responds positively to light. That is, it grows toward a light source such as the sun. Most stems grow upward, carrying the leaves toward the available light, which is needed by the leaves to make food. But if the light comes from one side, as from a window, the stem bends toward that light source.

The next time you see a wall covered with ivy, look closely at the leaves. The wall may be completely covered, but the ivy leaves do not cover one another. The stalk of each leaf actually bends so that each leaf can face the sun.

Some plants react to changes from day to night. The leaves of some impatiens spread out during the day, then droop at night. Oxalis flowers open at night, then close when morning comes.

Responding to Changes in the Environment

Sundews are small flowering plants that live in swamps. Their leaves have long, sticky hairs. Like the Venus's-flytrap and other insect-eating plants, sundews react to touch. When an insect lands on a sundew leaf, it sticks to some of the hairs and becomes entangled. Leaf edges gradually bend inward, trapping the insect. Then the sundew produces chemicals that break down the insect's body, turning it into food for the plant.

Animal Senses

Animals learn about the world through sense organs, which help them find food, recognize mates, detect danger, and locate breeding grounds.

There are five basic animal senses: sight, hearing, smell, taste, and touch. Certain senses are usually more highly developed than other senses. The crayfish, for example, has well-developed senses of touch, taste, and smell—but its sight and hearing are poor.

Sometimes you can guess which senses are the most important to an animal simply by looking at it.

In the Right Direction

People who hike in woods often carry a compass. The compass can be used to find direction. A small magnet in the compass, in the shape of a thin needle, is attracted to the Earth's magnetism. The needle points to the Earth's magnetic North Pole. This helps people orient themselves, so they can walk in a particular direction.

Many living things can also sense the Earth's magnetism. Homing pigeons orient themselves and navigate by sensing the Earth's magnetic force. So might bacteria, mollusks, honeybees, and salmon. These organisms have biological magnets made of a mineral called magnetite.

Recently, scientists discovered tiny crystals of magnetite in the human brain. Does this mean that people have a magnetic sense? Scientists do not know. But some people have exceptional navigational talents. Early Native American peoples, for example, traveled from place to place without maps, landmarks, compasses, or other navigational aids. Perhaps they had a magnetic sense of direction.

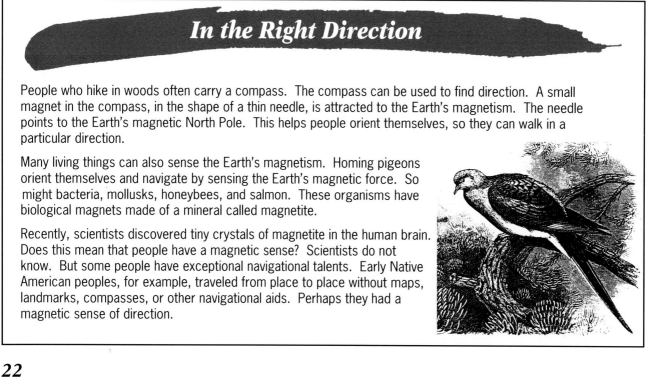

Rabbits have very long ears that can be moved from side to side to quickly locate the source of a sound. Rabbit survival is very dependent on hearing and recognizing sounds.

Many animals have senses that are much better developed than in humans. For example, a human nose has about 10 million scent receptors. This sounds like an enormous number, but it is not very much when compared to the nose of a Labrador retriever. The retriever has about 200 million scent receptors in its nose! Humans have made use of the retriever's fantastic nose. They have trained retrievers to sniff for bombs, drugs, termites, and gas leaks.

Many sense organs, including eyes, ears, noses, and antennae, are located on animal heads. But other parts of the body may also have sense organs. For

Animals take in information from their surroundings through their sense organs. The long barbels on the front of many fish are not only sensitive to touch, but are also able to relay taste messages to help them find food.

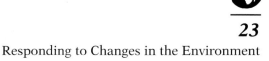

Like the barbels on a fish, long, projecting organs called antennae are used by crustaceans (like this spiny lobster, *right*) and insects (like this emperor moth, *below*) to detect sound, smell, touch, and taste stimuli in their surroundings.

Bacteria Hysteria

Scientists believe that there are millions of species of living things that have not yet been identified. Most of these species live in jungles, deep oceans, and other places that have not been explored.

Recently, scientists found a previously unknown kind of bacterium in the intestines of certain fish. These bacteria are much bigger than any other kind of bacteria ever seen. All other bacteria are microscopic, but this species is more than 0.02 inch (0.5 millimeter) long—still tiny (about the size of the period that ends this sentence), but easily seen without use of a microscope.

example, one kind of catfish has taste buds over its entire body. Some species of crickets even have "ears" on their legs!

Sense organs usually work together. The scallop—a mollusk that lives on the ocean floor—has about 40 bright blue eyes around the edge of its body. When the eyes see something of interest, the scallop extends its tentacles. The tentacles are covered with sense organs that can detect smells. Similarly, when sense organs on your foot feel pain, your eyes look down to see what is causing the pain. There also may be several responses to a stimulus. You may respond to pain in your foot by moving the foot, rubbing it, and shouting "Ouch!"

Animals of different species will sometimes live together, taking advantage of one another's senses. On the African plains, ostriches may live among groups of zebras and antelopes. The tall ostriches have huge eyes. They stand guard, watching out for lions and other predators. In return, the actions of the zebras and antelopes help the ostriches find food. As the zebras and antelopes eat grass, they uncover insects and reptiles, which are eaten by the ostriches.

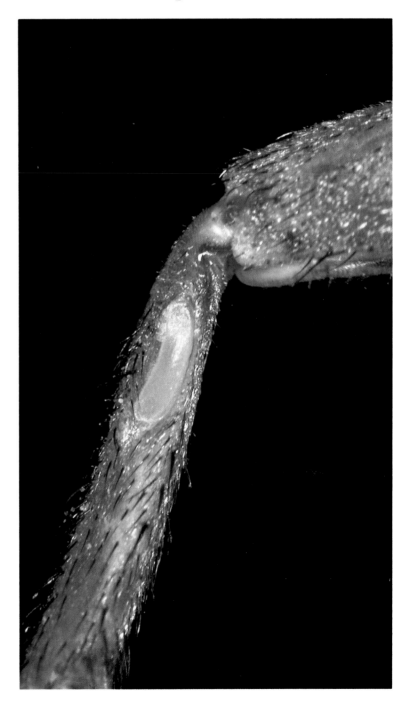

Some species of crickets have ear-like organs called tympanums on their legs. This organ, which is very similar to the human eardrum, is stimulated by the vibrations of sound waves.

3

Metabolism: How Living Things Function

A puddle of water that stays on the ground for several days quickly fills with life. If you looked at a drop of the water under a microscope, you would see all sorts of creatures. Some of the most active creatures would probably be one-celled parameciums.

Parameciums are fast movers relative to other organisms their size. They may move 0.1 inch (3 millimeters) a second and keep up this speed for hours. A paramecium moving at this speed is like a car traveling at 100 miles (160 kilometers) an hour! Moving so fast requires lots of energy. A car gets its energy from gasoline. A paramecium gets its energy from food. Parameciums feed mostly on bacteria. One paramecium may eat as many as 1,500 bacteria an hour!

Getting food, digesting it, and breaking it down for energy involves many chemical processes. Taken together, these processes—plus all the other chemical processes that take place in a living organism—are called metabolism. Metabolism is essential for life. When metabolism stops, an organism dies.

Opposite:
All living things must obtain food, digest it, and break it down for energy as part of a process called metabolism. Here, a southern alligator lizard feeds on a recently caught cricket.

A Thorough Burrow

The earthworm is one of the most important animals on Earth. Farmers call it "nature's plow." As earthworms burrow through the soil, they create spaces for air and water. Bacteria and other helpful soil organisms need the air and water to survive.

Earthworms swallow great amounts of soil. They also digest bits of roots and other food in the soil. The rest of the material passes through their digestive system. It is excreted on the surface in little heaps known as castings, which then help enrich the soil.

Energy from the Sun

Like parameciums, many organisms get their food by eating other organisms. But two groups of organisms—green plants and algae—make their own food. The food-making process is called photosynthesis, a word that means "putting together (synthesis) with light." During photosynthesis, carbon dioxide and water are "put together" to make food. Sunlight is the source of energy for this process.

Only cells that contain a green chemical called chlorophyll can carry out the process of photosynthesis. The chlorophyll is contained in tiny structures called chloroplasts. Photosynthesis takes place within the chloroplasts. Then the food is carried to other parts of the plant or alga. Some of the food is used immediately. It is used for energy, to build cells, and to reproduce. Extra food is stored for future use. For example, carrot and turnip plants store most extra food in their roots; celery plants store food in their leafstalks.

The Process of Photosynthesis

To make its own food, a green plant needs three ingredients: water, carbon dioxide, and energy from light.

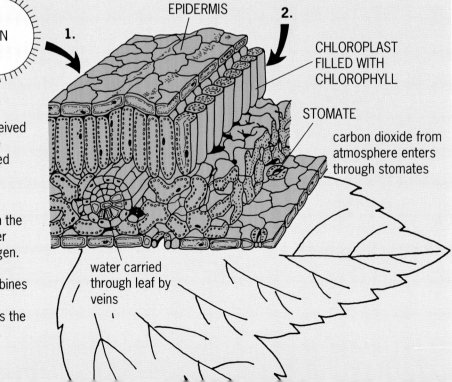

1. Light energy from the sun is received by chlorophyll and trapped in the chloroplasts, which have collected water from the veins and carbon dioxide from the air.

2. Light energy causes the water in the chloroplasts to break into simpler components: hydrogen and oxygen. The oxygen is released into the atmosphere. The hydrogen combines with the carbon dioxide to form glucose, a simple sugar, which is the simplest food.

EPIDERMIS

2.

SUN

1.

CHLOROPLAST FILLED WITH CHLOROPHYLL

STOMATE

carbon dioxide from atmosphere enters through stomates

water carried through leaf by veins

Animals and other organisms that cannot make their own food must eat plants and algae—or they must eat organisms that ate plants and algae. Green plants live mainly on land. They are the main source of food for most land-dwelling animals. Algae live mostly in water. They are the main source of food for many animals in oceans, lakes, and rivers.

How Animals Get Food

The food eaten by an animal depends on the kind of animal it is. Some animals, such as cows and grasshoppers, eat only green plants. Others, such as jellyfish and killer whales, eat only animals. Still others, such as bluebirds and snapping turtles, eat both plants and animals.

The shape of an animal's mouth gives a clue to its diet. The powerful bill of a parrot is designed for crushing hard seeds. The eagle's sharp, hooked bill is designed for tearing flesh. The butterfly's straw-like mouthparts are ideal for sipping liquids.

Some animals depend on their mouths to capture food. A frog flips out its tongue with lightning speed to grab a fly. A lamprey attaches itself by means of its sucker mouth to another fish, then drains the body fluids of its victim.

Many spiders build traps to catch their food. A silver Argiope builds a large, delicate-looking web between two branches of a bush. Then it sits quietly in the center of the web. When an insect lands on the web, it is caught by the sticky

Looking at an animal's features can tell you a lot about its lifestyle and diet. The long, spear-like bill of the stork (*below, left*) is perfect for catching fish. The sharp, hooked bill of the vulture (*below, middle*) is best adapted for tearing and eating meat. A chisel-shaped bill, like that of the woodpecker (*below, right*) is most effective for chipping away at wood.

Many animals, such as sea otters and chimpanzees, are tool-users. The best tool-users are humans, who have invented many effective ways to grow and catch large amounts of food for themselves and others.

threads. The spider is soon upon its victim, killing it by injecting venom into the body.

Some animals are tool-users. A sea otter uses a rock as a tool. It places the rock on its chest, then breaks clam shells by pounding them against the rock. A chimpanzee uses sticks and blades of grass as tools. It uses the stick to poke a hole in a termite nest. Next, it pushes the stick or a blade of grass deep into the hole. When the stick or blade of grass is inserted, termites cling to it and bite it. Then the chimp pulls the tool out and licks off the termites.

The best tool-users are humans. We use tools for many purposes, including getting food. We use shovels, plows, tractors, and many other tools to raise and harvest crops. We use milking machines to milk cows, knives to butcher animals, and vast nets to catch fish.

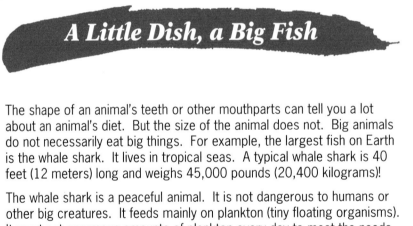

A Little Dish, a Big Fish

The shape of an animal's teeth or other mouthparts can tell you a lot about an animal's diet. But the size of the animal does not. Big animals do not necessarily eat big things. For example, the largest fish on Earth is the whale shark. It lives in tropical seas. A typical whale shark is 40 feet (12 meters) long and weighs 45,000 pounds (20,400 kilograms)!

The whale shark is a peaceful animal. It is not dangerous to humans or other big creatures. It feeds mainly on plankton (tiny floating organisms). It must eat enormous amounts of plankton every day to meet the needs of its huge body.

The whale shark's mouth is filled with thousands of tiny hooked teeth. Each jaw has more than 300 rows of teeth, with hundreds of teeth in each row. The gills at the back of the mouth are covered with a mesh.

To feed, the whale shark opens its wide mouth and swims through water that is filled with plankton. As the water passes through the whale shark's mouth, the plankton are trapped by the teeth and the mesh. The water passes through the gills and back out into the sea. Then, the whale shark closes its mouth. Gulp! The food is swallowed.

Releasing the Energy of Foods

Once food is in an organism's body, it is broken down into simpler substances. This process is called digestion. Some of the digested food is used to repair cells or to grow new cells. Some combines with oxygen to produce energy in a process called respiration.

Green plants and algae release large amounts of oxygen as a by-product of photosynthesis. Most of the oxygen is released into the air or water. The rest stays in the plants and algae so that they can respire.

All animals absorb oxygen from their environment. In sponges, corals, and other small animals that live in water, oxygen passes directly from the water into the cells of the body. Larger animals have special respiratory organs that take in oxygen. For example, mammals have lungs and fish have gills. Walls inside the lungs and gills are very thin. Oxygen passes through the walls and into the blood. The blood then carries the oxygen throughout the body.

Removing Wastes

During respiration, while food is broken down for energy, certain wastes are produced. These wastes have to be removed from the organism or else they will kill the organism.

One waste product of respiration in animals is carbon dioxide, which is removed, or excreted, from the organism. After the carbon dioxide has returned to the environment, it can be used by algae and green plants as a raw material for photosynthesis.

As you can see, there is a never-ending flow of chemicals from one organism to another. A carbon atom may pass through an oak tree, a caterpillar, a robin, and a hawk, then return to the air for awhile before it is absorbed by a corn plant and then eaten by a human.

How Fishes Breathe

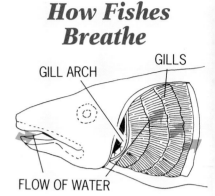

Most fishes have four gills on each side of the head. Water enters the mouth and flows out through the gills. Each gill is made up of fleshy, thread-like filaments.

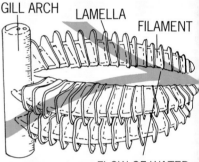

Water from the mouth passes over the filaments, which are closely spaced along a gill arch in two rows. Three of the many filaments of a gill are shown above.

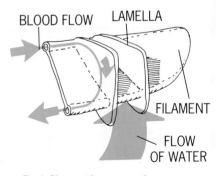

Each filament has many tiny extensions called lamellae. Blood flowing through a lamella takes oxygen from the water and releases carbon dioxide into the water.

4

Reproduction and Growth

 During the day, leopard frogs rest in hiding places near a small pond. As night begins, the male frogs leave their hiding places, moving into the pond. Each male has his own spot, or calling station, in the pond. Once there, he breathes in large amounts of air. He fills his lungs and puffs up pouches on the sides of his head. As he forces the air out of the lungs and pouches, he produces a loud call.

Female leopard frogs, their bodies swollen with eggs, recognize the calls of the male frogs and move toward the males. When a female reaches a male, he puts his front legs around her as she releases eggs into the water. At the same time, the male releases cells called sperm. When a sperm joins with an egg, a new life begins to form.

The female leopard frog may lay 6,000 eggs. Even if all of the eggs are fertilized by sperm, most of them

Opposite:
Newborn yellow warbler chicks await food from their parents. The process of reproduction is essential to all living things because it keeps each species in existence.

Out of the Skin You're In

At least once a year, a snake sheds the outside layer of its skin in a process called molting. The old layer is replaced by a new layer that forms underneath. The snake crawls right out of the old skin, turning it inside-out like the finger of a glove. Then the snake may eat the old skin. Some scientists believe the snake eats the skin for the protein it contains. Other scientists suggest that eating the skin protects the snake from enemies; eating destroys the evidence that the snake is nearby.

An amoeba reproduces by a method of asexual reproduction called binary fission. In this process, it is able to divide itself in half in order to create two new amoebas.

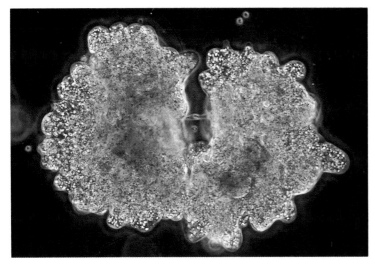

never hatch. Hungry fish and other predators eat them. But a few of the eggs survive, hatch, and develop into new leopard frogs.

This process of producing more organisms of the same kind is called reproduction. It is one of life's most important processes because it helps to keep a species alive. It does not matter if one leopard frog cannot reproduce. But if all leopard frogs were unable to reproduce, the species would soon become extinct. That means there would be no more leopard frogs on Earth.

One Parent or Two?

There are two kinds of reproduction. Individuals of some species can reproduce without a mate; this is called asexual reproduction. Usually, however, two parents are needed for reproduction; this is called sexual reproduction.

Asexual reproduction This method involves only one parent and is simple and fast. The offspring look exactly like the parent because they receive all their genes from that parent.

Bacteria, amoebas, and many other one-celled organisms can reproduce by dividing in half. This can happen very quickly. Bacteria can divide every 20 minutes when conditions are favorable.

Hydras, which are small relatives of jellyfish, can reproduce by budding. A tiny bud forms on the hydra's body. As the bud grows, tentacles and a mouth appear. When the bud has developed into a complete new hydra, it breaks off from the parent.

Bread mold is one of many kinds of fungi that reproduce asexually by spores. A spore consists of a single cell surrounded by a protective coat. The mold releases millions of spores into the air. If a spore lands in a favorable environment, it will develop.

Sexual reproduction This method of reproduction is more complicated than asexual reproduction, but it also is much more common. It involves two organisms—a male and a female. As in the case of the leopard frog, the male produces special cells called sperm. The female produces cells called eggs. Sperm and eggs must meet for reproduction to occur. A sperm cell must join with an egg cell to produce a new organism.

An organism that forms as a result of sexual reproduction receives half of its genes from the male parent and half from the female parent. It resembles

Bread mold is a kind of fungus that reproduces asexually with spores. The spores are single-celled reproductive agents that plant themselves in favorable environments in order to grow.

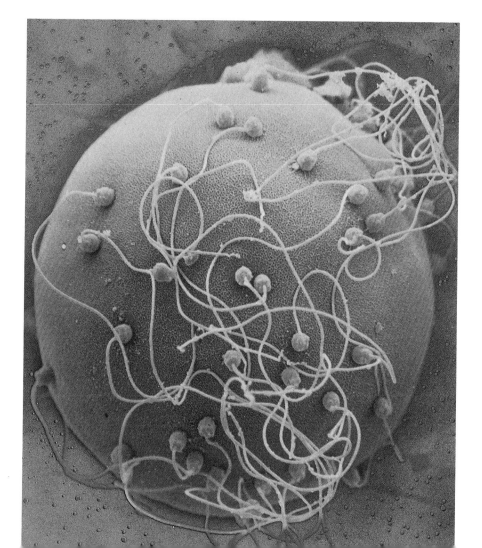

Most animals reproduce sexually in a process that requires sperm from a male and an egg from a female. Here, a microphotograph shows a human egg surrounded by a group of long-tailed sperm.

Crustaceans, such as lobsters, reproduce sexually, but the eggs are not released or fertilized for many months after mating.

DID YOU KNOW

The Bean Scene

Like all seeds, a bean has three parts: an outer coat, a supply of food, and an embryo. A bean embryo looks like a miniature plant, with a tiny root and two tiny leaves. To examine a bean embryo, soak a bean in water overnight. Carefully remove the seed coat. You will see that the bean has two halves. These contain all the stored food. Between the two halves is the embryo. Use a magnifying glass to get a close look.

both parents, but it does not look exactly like either of the parents.

Some species can reproduce only by sexual means. Others, such as bacteria, hydras, and fungi, are able to reproduce both sexually and asexually.

Flower Power

Most plants have special reproductive organs called flowers. Flowers come in many sizes, colors, and shapes. Some are large and brilliantly colored, others are so tiny that you will not notice them unless you search for them. All flowers, however, have the same purpose: to make seeds.

The male parts of flowers produce sperm, which are contained in tiny grains of pollen. The female parts of flowers produce eggs. Seeds develop after pollen from the male part of a plant is transferred to the female part of a plant in a process called pollination. The most common form of pollination is the transfer of pollen from one flower to another.

Plants have interesting adaptations for getting pollen from one flower to another. Many plants depend on insects. These plants have flowers with bright colors or strong odors. Insects are attracted by the colors and smells, and come to feed on sweet nectar and pollen. As an insect feeds, some of the pollen sticks to hairs on its body. When the insect moves to another flower of the same species, some of the pollen rubs off onto the flower's female parts.

Many other plants, including most species of grasses, depend on wind for pollination. They have small flowers, often without petals. Because their pollen weighs very little, the wind can carry it over long distances.

After a pollen grain reaches the female part of a flower, the next step is fertilization—the joining of the sperm and egg. The fertilized egg grows and becomes a seed. In time, the seed may fall to the ground. Often, however, it is carried by wind, water, or animals to a new location. The seed remains in a resting stage until conditions for growth are favorable. Then it sprouts, or germinates, and grows into a new plant.

Something in the Air

Many people suffer from hay fever. This is an allergic reaction to the pollen of certain plants. Symptoms include sneezing, an itchy nose, and red eyes. There are spring, summer, and fall kinds of hay fever, each caused by different kinds of pollen.

Most hay fever is caused by wind-pollinated plants. These plants shed enormous amounts of pollen into the air. Most of the pollen lands in unsuitable places. Very little reaches the female parts of flowers from the same species.

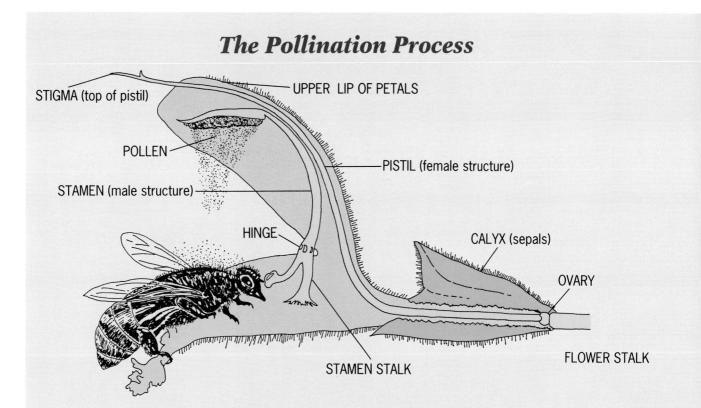

The Pollination Process

STIGMA (top of pistil)

UPPER LIP OF PETALS

POLLEN

PISTIL (female structure)

STAMEN (male structure)

HINGE

CALYX (sepals)

OVARY

STAMEN STALK

FLOWER STALK

The bee's head hits the stamen lever, which causes pollen to fall onto the bee's body. The bee will then travel to other flowers of the same kind. Some of the pollen falls off the bee onto the top of these flowers' pistils, pollinating them.

Animal Mates

Among animals, the first step in sexual reproduction is meeting a mate. In a sense, this has the same purpose as pollination in flowering plants: to bring sperm and eggs together.

Finding and attracting a member of the opposite sex is called courtship. Courtship behavior differs from species to species. The ability to sense and react to stimuli plays an important role. Many animals, like the leopard frog, depend on sound. Each species has its own special sounds, so that males and females can recognize one another.

Some animals have brilliant colors that they use to attract mates. During most of the year, the male stickleback has a silver belly. But when this small fish is ready to mate, his belly turns bright red. The male

Visual and aural (sound) stimulation seems to be an almost universal aspect to the mating rituals of animals. *Below:* thousands of fireflies swarm in a field, using a special flashing-light display to attract their mates. *Opposite, left:* This male egret displays long plumes that visually stimulate females when he is ready to mate. *Opposite, right:* The male American toad puffs out an impressive vocal sac that summons a mate and provides a dramatic visual display as well.

frigate bird has a sac on his throat that is normally pale pink. At mating time, the sac turns bright red; the male forces air into the sac, making it very big.

Chemical signals are used by many species to bring males and females together. When a female emperor butterfly is ready to mate, she releases special chemicals into the air. When a male emperor butterfly senses the odor of these chemicals, he will follow the trail until he reaches the female.

During mating, a male releases sperm. Sperm usually swim through a liquid to reach and fertilize an egg. Most animals that live in water shed their eggs and sperm into water. The sperm swim toward the eggs and fertilize them. Among land animals, eggs are usually fertilized inside the female's body. For example, among birds and mammals, the male releases a fluid containing sperm into an opening to the female's reproductive system. The sperm then

DID YOU KNOW

Gifted Ones

Young men often give their girlfriends flowers. Males of some other species also bring gifts to females. A male wolf spider will often capture a fly and wrap it in silk before giving it to a mate. A male Adélie penguin will offer a stone to a female. Male terns are known to bring a fish and place it directly in the female's mouth. Now that's service!

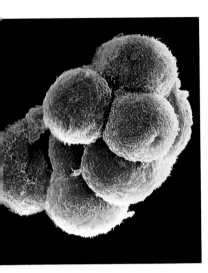

Only 4 days after fertilization, the human egg has multiplied into 16 cells.

A mass of fertilized lobster eggs clings to the uropod of a female lobster until they are ready to hatch.

swim toward the egg. When an egg and sperm join together, the egg is said to be fertilized. Like a plant seed, it contains everything needed to develop into a new individual.

Stages of Life

After fertilization, the egg of a plant or animal divides again and again. Soon, the one cell has become hundreds of cells. This mass of cells is called an embryo. At first, all the cells of an embryo are exactly alike. But soon, cells begin to specialize. In a sunflower embryo, for example, some cells become root cells and others become stem cells. In a monkey embryo some cells become muscle cells and others become blood cells.

Growth continues after birth. A sunflower seedling develops into a tall plant—if it has enough sunlight, water, and carbon dioxide to make lots of food. A

An oak tree may produce 10,000 acorns in one year. A lobster may lay 15,000 eggs at a time. A Virginia oyster may release 50 million eggs at a time! Most acorns, lobster eggs, and oyster eggs never develop into mature organisms. Instead, they are eaten or killed by unfavorable environmental conditions.

In comparison, a field sparrow lays four or five eggs. A female cat may give birth to four or five kittens. A female human usually gives birth to one baby at a time. Most baby sparrows, cats, and humans grow up to become adults. They survive because their parents give them lots of care.

Bird and mammal parents are some of the best parents on Earth. They keep their babies warm and dry and feed their babies frequently. They wash their babies and get rid of their wastes. When the babies grow older, the parents teach them how to find food and how to communicate. For example, one of the most important things that a young sparrow learns from its parents are its songs. Similarly, a human baby learns language from its parents.

Newborn piglets nursing

monkey baby develops into an adult—also, only if its environmental conditions are favorable.

Most animals grow bigger for a limited period of time. For example, humans grow taller until they are in their late teens. Many plants, however, continue to grow until they die. Some redwood trees in California are 2,000 years old—and still growing taller!

Many animals, such as the lobster and this nursery web spider, carry their fertilized eggs with them so they remain protected as they develop.

5

Fitting into the Web of Life

 Remember the last time you walked in a park? Think of all the living things you saw! There were probably grasses, small flowering plants, and various kinds of bushes and trees. Birds, squirrels, and insects sat in the trees or walked on the ground. If there was a pond, it may have contained fish, frogs, and even a snake or two. Of course, there were many organisms in the park that you did not see, such as worms and fungi that live underground.

All these organisms live in the park because it contains everything they need to live and grow. The park is their home, or habitat. Each organism has adaptations that help it survive in the park. Some of these adaptations help in finding food or mates. Others help the organisms raise their young or defend themselves against enemies and bad weather.

Opposite:
All living things are interconnected in one way or another. This pollen-covered flower beetle, for example, gets food from the daisy before it carries the flower's pollen off to another daisy for possible pollination.

Perhaps the park has changed since you last walked there. Perhaps a meadow was turned into a baseball field, or trees were cut down to make a playground. When habitats change, the organisms that live there are affected. Some of the organisms are able to adjust and survive in the new habitat, but others simply cannot adjust.

Eating...and Being Eaten

In most habitats, there are algae or green plants that turn light energy into food energy. As the algae or plants are eaten, the energy is passed on to another organism. This flow of energy from one organism to another is called a food chain. An example of a food chain is a robin eating a caterpillar that ate leaves of a maple tree. Another food chain is a dolphin eating a squid that ate small fish that ate one-celled algae.

A food chain continues when an organism dies. Certain bacteria and fungi get their energy by breaking down the remains of dead organisms. As the bacteria and fungi work, important chemicals are returned to the soil or water. Green plants and algae can use these chemicals to make food.

A habitat contains hundreds of food chains that crisscross and overlap in a network called a food web. Robins eat worms as well as caterpillars, and caterpillars are preyed on by many different kinds of birds. Dolphins eat fish as well as squid. Humans eat meat from pigs, sheep, and many other organisms.

Eating a variety of foods is a valuable adaptation. If one food source disappears, the organism can eat something else. Organisms that depend on a single source of food may starve if that food disappears. Pandas live in bamboo forests and eat only bamboo leaves and shoots. As people cut down the forests, the pandas die.

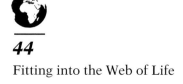

A Typical Food Chain

A. Microscopic algae in a pond.

B. Protozoans eat the algae.

C. Small insects eat the protozoans.

D. Larger animals eat the smaller insects.

E. A bass eats the larger animals.

F. A human eats the bass.

Defense in the Natural World

Certain organisms may be very successful at making or getting food. They may be very successful at reproducing. But these abilities mean little if the organisms are easily killed by enemies. Staying alive is very important to the success of a species.

To stay alive, organisms have evolved ways to protect themselves. Indeed, most organisms have a variety of defenses. If one defense does not work, they try another. The graceful chameleon of central Africa tries to avoid enemies by blending into its background. If this does not work and it comes face to face with an enemy, the chameleon tries to scare it away by inflating its body and hissing.

In order to survive, all organisms have ways of defending themselves in the natural world. The porcupine (*above*) and the stinging nettle (*below*) both use sharp, pointed spines to prevent enemies from getting too close.

If a species cannot defend itself, it is likely to become extinct. The Javan rhinoceros, which lives in swampy jungles on an island in Indonesia, has two sharp, pointed tusks. These tusks are excellent weapons against natural enemies. But the tusks are not enough

Let's Spore S'more

Humans aren't the only farmers. Some ants are also expert farmers. Atta ants cultivate fungus gardens for food. Just like human farmers, ant farmers begin by preparing the garden's "soil." Then they sow and care for the crop. Finally, they harvest it and feed upon it.

The ants climb trees near their nest and cut off pieces of leaves. They carry the pieces to a special room in the nest. They chew the pieces and deposit them on the floor of the room. When this "soil" is ready, the ants plant the spores of certain fungi. Soon the garden is covered with the thin threads of fungi.

Some of the ants spend most of their lives taking care of the garden and "weeding" out unwanted organisms. Before long, reproductive structures develop on the fungi. The farmer ants then bite off these structures and feed them to other ants in the nest.

to protect the rhinos against humans, who can kill them with guns and destroy the jungles, leaving the rhinos without homes and food.

Here are some examples of how organisms protect themselves against enemies:

Structural defenses Built-in defenses help many organisms to stay alive. The soft bodies of most mollusks are protected by hard shells. Remove a snail, clam, or other mollusk from its shell and it will die. The box turtle would also die without its shell. When danger threatens, this turtle can pull itself completely inside the shell. Plants such as peach trees produce seeds with very hard outer coverings. This protects the seeds against hungry animals.

Spines and thorns are another kind of structural defense. Cactus plants, rosebushes, sea urchins, and porcupines are among the organisms that depend on these structures to keep away hungry animals.

For many animals, a valuable defense is speed. Deer, kangaroos, and rabbits have strong leg muscles that help them escape their enemies. When danger threatens on land, ducks and other birds depend on strong muscles to carry them quickly into the air.

Many organisms use their structural defenses to help them stay alive. The armadillo (*below, left*) and the stinkpot turtle (*below, right*) are both protected from enemies by tough shells.

Camouflage—blending into the surroundings—is one of the most effective means of defense for many living things. The Malaysian leaf frog (*top*) is a master at blending into its surroundings; so is the bittern (*above, left*) and the stonefish (*above, right*).

Camouflage The color and shape of some organisms help them to blend into the environment. This camouflage hides the organisms from their enemies—and from the prey they hope to catch. The walking stick is a slow-moving, brownish insect that looks like a twig. The green mamba is a snake that lives on leafy tree branches in African forests.

Fitting into the Web of Life

Some organisms can even change their colors as the environment changes. The flounder is a flat fish that can change color to match the shifting sands on which it rests. A ptarmigan, a bird that lives in the Arctic, has brown feathers in summer and snow-white feathers in winter.

Chemical warfare Poisons are an important means of self-defense for many organisms. Amanita mushrooms produce poisons that can be deadly to humans and other animals who eat them. The leaves of poison ivy contain a poison that causes itchy blisters on people who touch them. The Atlantic stingray has a barbed spine on the top surface of its whip-like tail. If a human or other creature touches the stingray, the spine plunges into the attacker's skin as poison flows through two grooves in the spine.

Bluffing When an enemy comes near a Tokay gecko, this lizard tries to get rid of the enemy by bluffing. It arches its back to look bigger and opens

Many organisms produce powerful poisons to discourage predators. Both the brightly colored arrow-poison frog (*below, left*) and the brightly colored amanita mushroom (*below, right*) produce potent toxins that can harm humans and other animals.

The frilled lizard (*below, left*) and the pufferfish (*below, right*) are just two of the many animals that can change their appearance in order to "bluff" or scare away possible enemies.

its mouth to show off the pink and black lining. It even barks! If the enemy is not scared off, the Tokay gecko stops bluffing and rushes forward to bite the enemy.

Adapting to a Changing Environment

Various conditions in an environment constantly change. Every 24 hours there is a change from day to night. In some environments, hot summers are followed by cold winters. Elsewhere, rainy seasons are followed by dry seasons. To survive, organisms must be able to adapt to such changes. Two common adaptations that help organisms survive changing environments are resting stages and migration.

Resting stages Many organisms enter resting stages to survive heat, dryness, freezing temperatures, or other unfavorable conditions. During a resting stage, body processes (metabolism) slow down. Very little energy is used.

Some bacteria survive unfavorable conditions, such as high temperatures and harmful chemicals, by forming structures called endospores. An endospore has a thick, waterproof coat that protects the delicate cytoplasm and nucleus. The organism stays in this

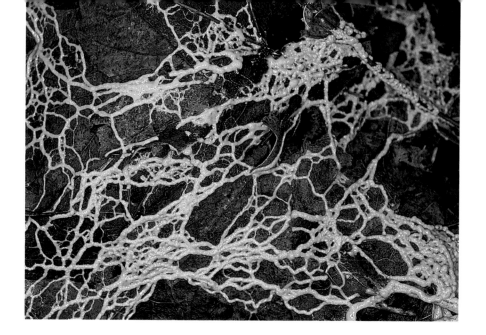

Many organisms react to unfavorable environmental conditions by entering a resting stage, when metabolism slows down significantly. Slime molds, such as the one above, thicken up and slow their movements when little or no water is available.

resting stage until it is in a favorable environment. Then the endospore takes in water and becomes an active bacterium.

Plants such as marigolds and peas are annuals; they live only one year. The seeds germinate in the spring, and the plants grow until they are killed by the onset of cold weather. Before this happens, however, they produce seeds that have a tough, waterproof coat. The seeds are the resting stage in the life cycle of annuals. They survive until environmental conditions are suitable for growth. The seeds of some annuals can survive for many years without losing their ability to germinate.

The African lungfish has lungs as well as gills. Although the lungfish takes in some oxygen through its gills, almost all of its oxygen is obtained by rising to the surface and breathing air. During the hot, dry season, the river in which it lives dries up. The lungfish survives by burrowing into the mud and entering a resting stage. It stays inside its ball of mud through the dry season. When the rainy season arrives, the lungfish breaks out of the mud and once again begins to swim about.

A frog—like other amphibians, insects, reptiles, birds, and mammals—can survive cold winters by

DID YOU KNOW

Loads of Toads

Sometimes, human efforts to improve the environment lead to disaster. One such example began in the early 1900s. Australian farmers looked for a way to get rid of grayback beetles, which were destroying the sugarcane crop. In 1934, they imported 102 cane toads from Hawaii. Cane toads love to eat insects. But grayback beetles live on the top of tall sugarcane plants. Cane toads live on the ground. The two never met. Still, the cane toads found many other things to eat. Today there are millions of cane toads in Australia. Now they are pests—just like the grayback beetles.

The Cave Rave

Green plants cannot live in caves because there is no light. But many animals live in caves. Where does their food come from?

Most caves have openings to the outside world. Bats, birds, and other animals feed in the outside world but use the caves as resting places. Their droppings provide food for other cave dwellers. When they die, still other cave dwellers feed on their carcasses (decomposing bodies). Even though there are no green plants or algae in the caves, the food chains start with these food-making organisms.

Millions of years ago, a cave in what is now Romania was cut off from the outside world when its opening was covered up by soil. Nothing could enter or leave the cave. Recently, people discovered the cave 60 feet (18 meters) below the Earth's surface. To their amazement, the cave was filled with life!

The animals in this cave are unlike any others ever seen. There are spiders without eyes, flies without wings, and leeches that suck fluids from worms instead of blood from other animals.

The cave is one of the few habitats on Earth where food chains do not begin with photosynthesis. The cave's food chains begin not with green plants or algae but with bacteria. Instead of using the sun's energy to make food, these bacteria take energy from a gas called hydrogen sulfide.

Blind cave salamander

Scientists believe that the ancestors of these strange cave dwellers were similar to organisms found elsewhere. As the cave was gradually sealed off, some organisms were able to adapt to the changing environment. Over millions of years, they evolved into new species.

DID YOU KNOW

Herd It Through the Grapevine

Animals that live in herds depend on one another for protection. Musk oxen are large, shaggy mammals that live in herds. Their main enemies are wolves. When a herd is threatened by wolves, it forms a circle. The young musk oxen are inside the circle. The adults face outward, toward the wolves. If the wolves do not leave, the adult musk oxen charge. They use their big horns and strong hoofs to stab and trample the wolves.

hibernating. It digs a hole in the mud at the bottom of a pond or in damp soil in the woods. It stays in the hole through the winter. During this time, the frog's heart slows down. Any oxygen it needs is absorbed through its skin. The frog does not eat, but it gets the energy it needs from fat stored in its body.

Migration In many parts of the world, winter brings icy temperatures. Food supplies are killed or become covered by thick layers of snow. Some animals adapt by moving to places that are warmer and have more abundant food supplies. This seasonal movement is called migration. Animals may migrate enormous distances. For example, the golden plover spends summers in northern Canada and winters in South America. Its round-trip migration route is more than 11,800 miles (19,000 kilometers) long!

Dryness may cause migration, too. Zebras, wilde-beests, and other grass-eaters in central Africa migrate from dry areas to areas where rain keeps the grass green. Animals that feed on the grass-eaters usually migrate, too.

Some sea animals also migrate. For instance, gray whales spend the summer in the Bering Sea and the Arctic Ocean. In autumn, they swim southward to spend the winter off the coast of Mexico.

Humans and Other Living Things

Humans depend on other living things in numerous ways. Farmers raise many kinds of plants and animals for food. Bacteria, fungi, and algae are also sources of human food. For example, a chemical taken from brown algae is used in ice cream, salad dressings, and pie fillings.

Humans obtain lumber, paper, rayon, rubber, and fuel from trees. We make clothing from the fibers of cotton and flax plants, and from the hair of sheep and goats. Many vital medicines come from bacteria and green plants.

Other living things also provide valuable services. Trees and grasses protect soil from erosion. Bacteria and fungi break down dead organisms.

Of course, some living things cause problems for humans. Certain bacteria, fungi, and worms cause diseases. Some blue-green algae can make water undrinkable. And many insects—known as pests—feed on people's crops.

At the same time, the human population is growing rapidly. Humans need more and more land on which to live and grow food. When grasslands are turned into towns for humans, the homes of many plants and animals are destroyed. The homes of other kinds of plants and animals are destroyed when

Humans rely on other living things for their existence (*above*). Plants and animals provide food, medicines, fuel, and many other essential products for human survival. Cotton (*below*) is just one plant that provides the material for human clothing and textiles.

Humans are connected to other living things in many different ways—most importantly because human activities directly affect the very existence of so many other organisms. Burning rainforests for commercial purposes (*above*) destroys habitats for thousands of plants and animals. Overhunting and habitat destruction also threaten or endanger many species, including the Galapagos tortoise (*below*), the resplendent quetzal (*right*) and the orangutan (*far right*).

forests are cut down to make room for farms, when lakes and swamps are filled to build parking lots and shopping centers, and when dams are built across rivers.

Because of human activities, many creatures face extinction. Blue whales and rhinoceroses are in danger of becoming extinct because of uncontrolled hunting. Pandas and koalas are dwindling in number because people are destroying their habitats. Many cacti have become rare because people uproot them from their homes.

More than any other species on Earth, humans can change the environment both positively and negatively. This gives humans great power, but it is important for us to use this power very carefully. We must always respect the environment and consider the impact of our actions. If we do, we can continue to enjoy the beauty and wonder of all the other organisms that share this planet and the processes of being alive with us.

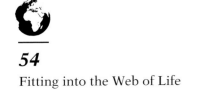

A Timeline of Life on Earth

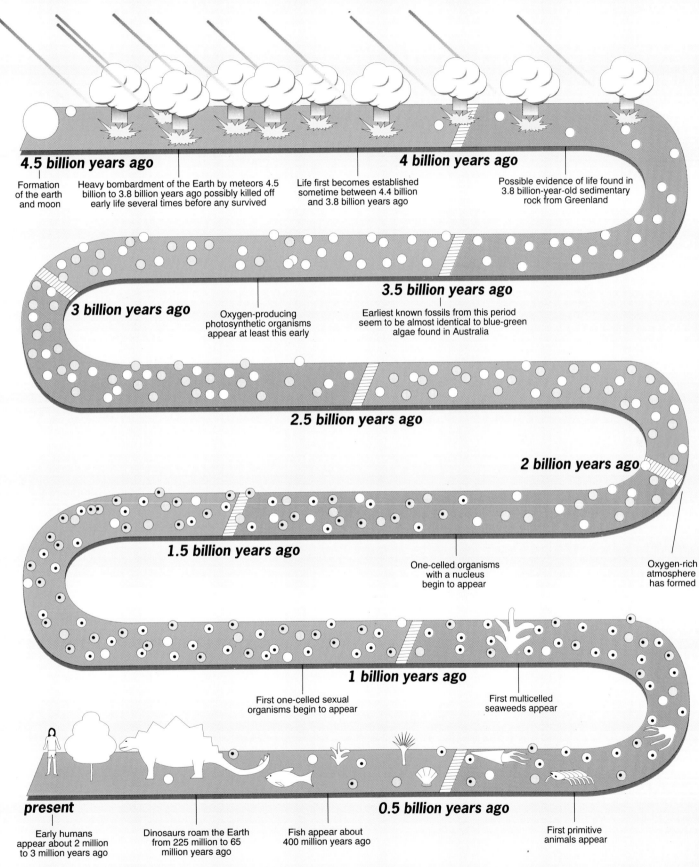

KINGDOM PROTISTA

KINGDOM FUNGI

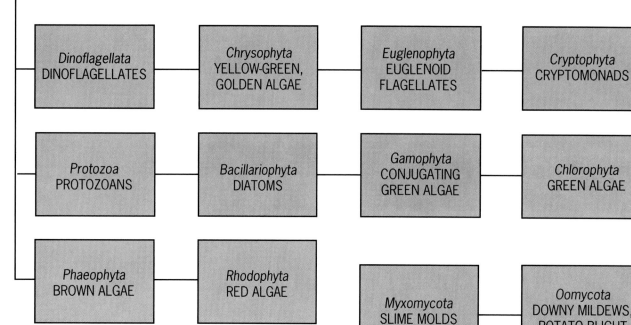

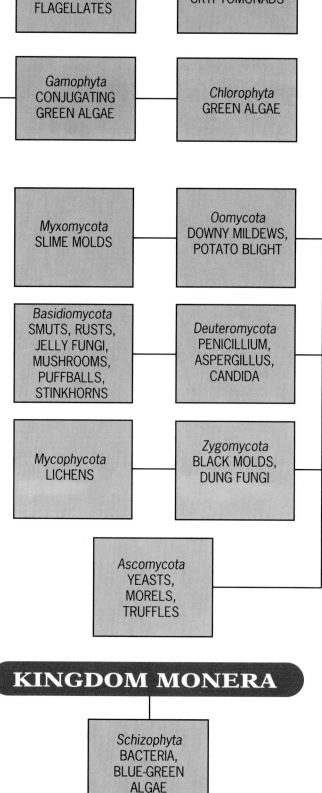

Dinoflagellata
DINOFLAGELLATES

Chrysophyta
YELLOW-GREEN,
GOLDEN ALGAE

Euglenophyta
EUGLENOID
FLAGELLATES

Cryptophyta
CRYPTOMONADS

Protozoa
PROTOZOANS

Bacillariophyta
DIATOMS

Gamophyta
CONJUGATING
GREEN ALGAE

Chlorophyta
GREEN ALGAE

Phaeophyta
BROWN ALGAE

Rhodophyta
RED ALGAE

Myxomycota
SLIME MOLDS

Oomycota
DOWNY MILDEWS,
POTATO BLIGHT

Basidiomycota
SMUTS, RUSTS,
JELLY FUNGI,
MUSHROOMS,
PUFFBALLS,
STINKHORNS

Deuteromycota
PENICILLIUM,
ASPERGILLUS,
CANDIDA

Mycophycota
LICHENS

Zygomycota
BLACK MOLDS,
DUNG FUNGI

Ascomycota
YEASTS,
MORELS,
TRUFFLES

KINGDOM MONERA

Schizophyta
BACTERIA,
BLUE-GREEN
ALGAE

Biological Classification

For a long time, plants were considered one of two kingdoms that classified all living things on Earth. The two kingdoms were the plant kingdom and the animal kingdom. As scientists studied the approximately 400,000 different kinds of plants, however, they began to realize that many did not fit well into either the plant or the animal kingdom. In response to this problem, scientists began to construct additional kingdoms into which they could put various groupings of life. The most recent trend in classification has been toward five kingdoms to classify all living things on Earth. Shown here are four kingdoms that—with the animal kingdom—make up a five-kingdom classification structure.

The four kingdoms shown here are the kingdom plantae (mosses, ferns, seed/flowering plants, and other minor groups), kingdom fungi (mushrooms and molds), kingdom protista (algae and protozoa), and kingdom monera (blue-green algae and bacteria). In any kingdom the hierarchy of classification is the same. As this chart shows, groupings go from the most general categories down to the more specific. The most general grouping shown here is PHYLUM (or DIVISION for plants). The most specific grouping listed is ORDER. To use the chart, you may want to find a familiar organism in a CLASS or ORDER box and then trace its classification upward until you reach its PHYLUM or DIVISION.

KINGDOM PLANTAE

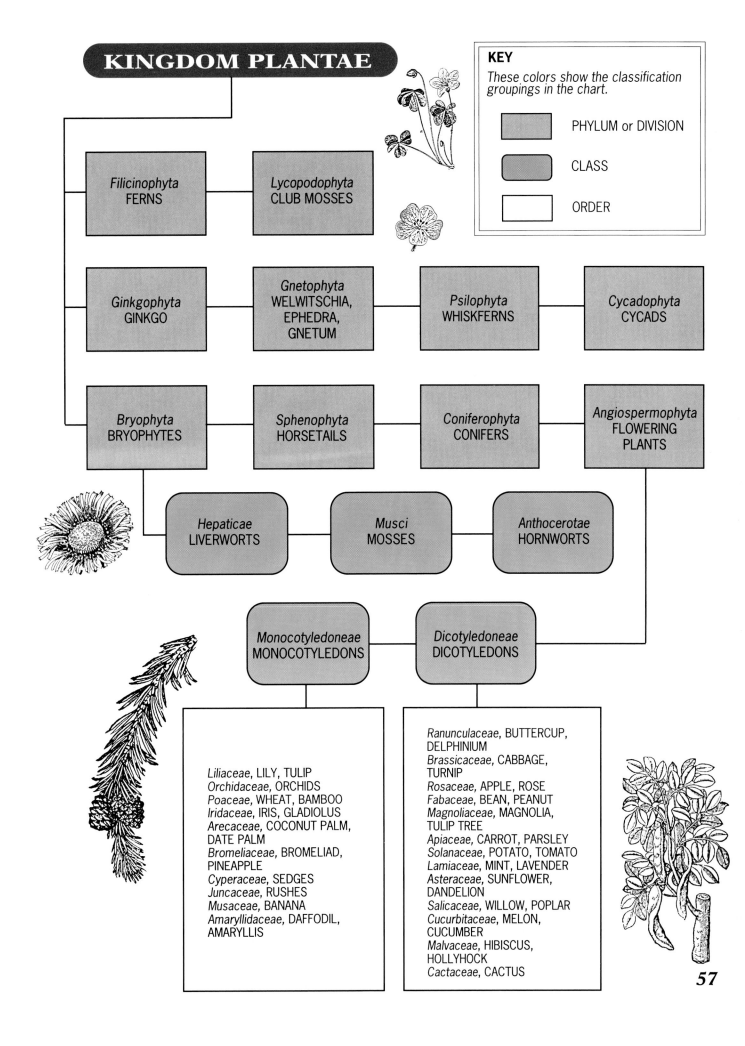

KEY
These colors show the classification groupings in the chart.

PHYLUM or DIVISION

CLASS

ORDER

Filicinophyta FERNS

Lycopodophyta CLUB MOSSES

Ginkgophyta GINKGO

Gnetophyta WELWITSCHIA, EPHEDRA, GNETUM

Psilophyta WHISKFERNS

Cycadophyta CYCADS

Bryophyta BRYOPHYTES

Sphenophyta HORSETAILS

Coniferophyta CONIFERS

Angiospermophyta FLOWERING PLANTS

Hepaticae LIVERWORTS

Musci MOSSES

Anthocerotae HORNWORTS

Monocotyledoneae MONOCOTYLEDONS

Dicotyledoneae DICOTYLEDONS

Liliaceae, LILY, TULIP
Orchidaceae, ORCHIDS
Poaceae, WHEAT, BAMBOO
Iridaceae, IRIS, GLADIOLUS
Arecaceae, COCONUT PALM, DATE PALM
Bromeliaceae, BROMELIAD, PINEAPPLE
Cyperaceae, SEDGES
Juncaceae, RUSHES
Musaceae, BANANA
Amaryllidaceae, DAFFODIL, AMARYLLIS

Ranunculaceae, BUTTERCUP, DELPHINIUM
Brassicaceae, CABBAGE, TURNIP
Rosaceae, APPLE, ROSE
Fabaceae, BEAN, PEANUT
Magnoliaceae, MAGNOLIA, TULIP TREE
Apiaceae, CARROT, PARSLEY
Solanaceae, POTATO, TOMATO
Lamiaceae, MINT, LAVENDER
Asteraceae, SUNFLOWER, DANDELION
Salicaceae, WILLOW, POPLAR
Cucurbitaceae, MELON, CUCUMBER
Malvaceae, HIBISCUS, HOLLYHOCK
Cactaceae, CACTUS

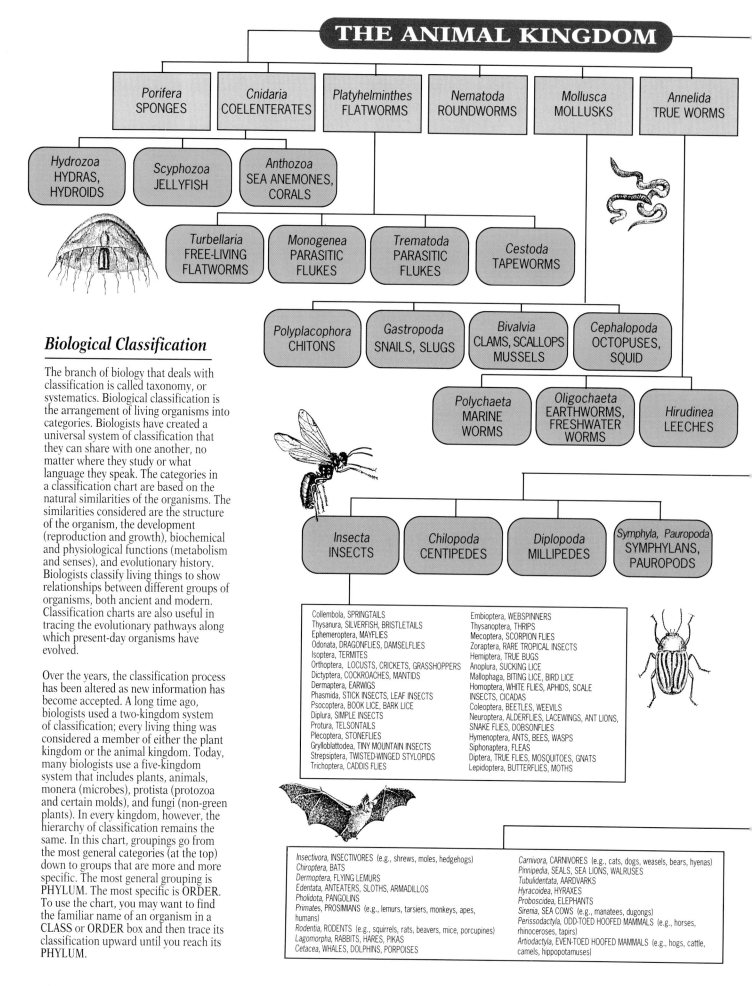

THE ANIMAL KINGDOM

| Porifera SPONGES | Cnidaria COELENTERATES | Platyhelminthes FLATWORMS | Nematoda ROUNDWORMS | Mollusca MOLLUSKS | Annelida TRUE WORMS |

Hydrozoa HYDRAS, HYDROIDS

Scyphozoa JELLYFISH

Anthozoa SEA ANEMONES, CORALS

Turbellaria FREE-LIVING FLATWORMS

Monogenea PARASITIC FLUKES

Trematoda PARASITIC FLUKES

Cestoda TAPEWORMS

Polyplacophora CHITONS

Gastropoda SNAILS, SLUGS

Bivalvia CLAMS, SCALLOPS MUSSELS

Cephalopoda OCTOPUSES, SQUID

Polychaeta MARINE WORMS

Oligochaeta EARTHWORMS, FRESHWATER WORMS

Hirudinea LEECHES

Biological Classification

The branch of biology that deals with classification is called taxonomy, or systematics. Biological classification is the arrangement of living organisms into categories. Biologists have created a universal system of classification that they can share with one another, no matter where they study or what language they speak. The categories in a classification chart are based on the natural similarities of the organisms. The similarities considered are the structure of the organism, the development (reproduction and growth), biochemical and physiological functions (metabolism and senses), and evolutionary history. Biologists classify living things to show relationships between different groups of organisms, both ancient and modern. Classification charts are also useful in tracing the evolutionary pathways along which present-day organisms have evolved.

Over the years, the classification process has been altered as new information has become accepted. A long time ago, biologists used a two-kingdom system of classification; every living thing was considered a member of either the plant kingdom or the animal kingdom. Today, many biologists use a five-kingdom system that includes plants, animals, monera (microbes), protista (protozoa and certain molds), and fungi (non-green plants). In every kingdom, however, the hierarchy of classification remains the same. In this chart, groupings go from the most general categories (at the top) down to groups that are more and more specific. The most general grouping is PHYLUM. The most specific is ORDER. To use the chart, you may want to find the familiar name of an organism in a CLASS or ORDER box and then trace its classification upward until you reach its PHYLUM.

Insecta INSECTS

Chilopoda CENTIPEDES

Diplopoda MILLIPEDES

Symphyla, Pauropoda SYMPHYLANS, PAUROPODS

Collembola, SPRINGTAILS
Thysanura, SILVERFISH, BRISTLETAILS
Ephemeroptera, MAYFLIES
Odonata, DRAGONFLIES, DAMSELFLIES
Isoptera, TERMITES
Orthoptera, LOCUSTS, CRICKETS, GRASSHOPPERS
Dictyptera, COCKROACHES, MANTIDS
Dermaptera, EARWIGS
Phasmida, STICK INSECTS, LEAF INSECTS
Psocoptera, BOOK LICE, BARK LICE
Diplura, SIMPLE INSECTS
Protura, TELSONTAILS
Plecoptera, STONEFLIES
Grylloblattodea, TINY MOUNTAIN INSECTS
Strepsiptera, TWISTED-WINGED STYLOPIDS
Trichoptera, CADDIS FLIES

Embioptera, WEBSPINNERS
Thysanoptera, THRIPS
Mecoptera, SCORPION FLIES
Zoraptera, RARE TROPICAL INSECTS
Hemiptera, TRUE BUGS
Anoplura, SUCKING LICE
Mallophaga, BITING LICE, BIRD LICE
Homoptera, WHITE FLIES, APHIDS, SCALE INSECTS, CICADAS
Coleoptera, BEETLES, WEEVILS
Neuroptera, ALDERFLIES, LACEWINGS, ANT LIONS, SNAKE FLIES, DOBSONFLIES
Hymenoptera, ANTS, BEES, WASPS
Siphonaptera, FLEAS
Diptera, TRUE FLIES, MOSQUITOES, GNATS
Lepidoptera, BUTTERFLIES, MOTHS

Insectivora, INSECTIVORES (e.g., shrews, moles, hedgehogs)
Chiroptera, BATS
Dermoptera, FLYING LEMURS
Edentata, ANTEATERS, SLOTHS, ARMADILLOS
Pholidota, PANGOLINS
Primates, PROSIMIANS (e.g., lemurs, tarsiers, monkeys, apes, humans)
Rodentia, RODENTS (e.g., squirrels, rats, beavers, mice, porcupines)
Lagomorpha, RABBITS, HARES, PIKAS
Cetacea, WHALES, DOLPHINS, PORPOISES

Carnivora, CARNIVORES (e.g., cats, dogs, weasels, bears, hyenas)
Pinnipedia, SEALS, SEA LIONS, WALRUSES
Tubulidentata, AARDVARKS
Hyracoidea, HYRAXES
Proboscidea, ELEPHANTS
Sirenia, SEA COWS (e.g., manatees, dugongs)
Perissodactyla, ODD-TOED HOOFED MAMMALS (e.g., horses, rhinoceroses, tapirs)
Artiodactyla, EVEN-TOED HOOFED MAMMALS (e.g., hogs, cattle, camels, hippopotamuses)

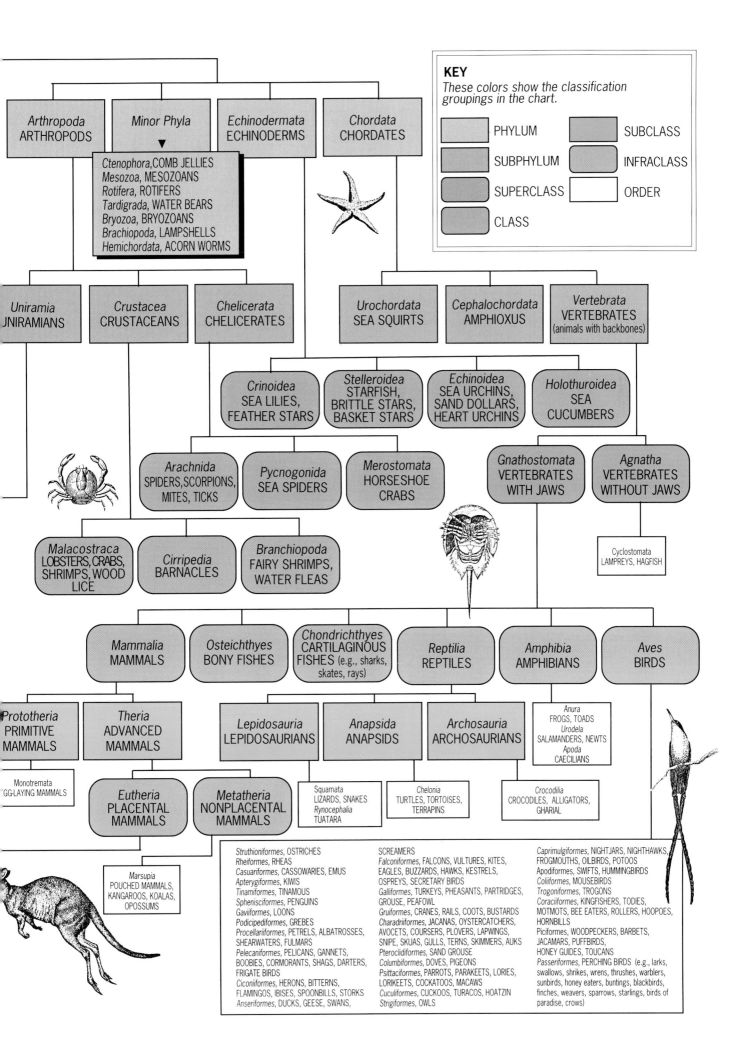

KEY
These colors show the classification groupings in the chart.

PHYLUM   SUBCLASS

SUBPHYLUM   INFRACLASS

SUPERCLASS   ORDER

CLASS

Arthropoda ARTHROPODS

Minor Phyla ▼

Ctenophora, COMB JELLIES
Mesozoa, MESOZOANS
Rotifera, ROTIFERS
Tardigrada, WATER BEARS
Bryozoa, BRYOZOANS
Brachiopoda, LAMPSHELLS
Hemichordata, ACORN WORMS

Echinodermata ECHINODERMS

Chordata CHORDATES

Uniramia UNIRAMIANS

Crustacea CRUSTACEANS

Chelicerata CHELICERATES

Urochordata SEA SQUIRTS

Cephalochordata AMPHIOXUS

Vertebrata VERTEBRATES (animals with backbones)

Crinoidea SEA LILIES, FEATHER STARS

Stelleroidea STARFISH, BRITTLE STARS, BASKET STARS

Echinoidea SEA URCHINS, SAND DOLLARS, HEART URCHINS

Holothuroidea SEA CUCUMBERS

Arachnida SPIDERS, SCORPIONS, MITES, TICKS

Pycnogonida SEA SPIDERS

Merostomata HORSESHOE CRABS

Gnathostomata VERTEBRATES WITH JAWS

Agnatha VERTEBRATES WITHOUT JAWS

Malacostraca LOBSTERS, CRABS, SHRIMPS, WOOD LICE

Cirripedia BARNACLES

Branchiopoda FAIRY SHRIMPS, WATER FLEAS

Cyclostomata LAMPREYS, HAGFISH

Mammalia MAMMALS

Osteichthyes BONY FISHES

Chondrichthyes CARTILAGINOUS FISHES (e.g., sharks, skates, rays)

Reptilia REPTILES

Amphibia AMPHIBIANS

Aves BIRDS

Prototheria PRIMITIVE MAMMALS

Theria ADVANCED MAMMALS

Lepidosauria LEPIDOSAURIANS

Anapsida ANAPSIDS

Archosauria ARCHOSAURIANS

Anura FROGS, TOADS
Urodela SALAMANDERS, NEWTS
Apoda CAECILIANS

Monotremata EGG-LAYING MAMMALS

Eutheria PLACENTAL MAMMALS

Metatheria NONPLACENTAL MAMMALS

Squamata LIZARDS, SNAKES
Rynocephalia TUATARA

Chelonia TURTLES, TORTOISES, TERRAPINS

Crocodilia CROCODILES, ALLIGATORS, GHARIAL

Marsupia POUCHED MAMMALS, KANGAROOS, KOALAS, OPOSSUMS

Struthioniformes, OSTRICHES
Rheiformes, RHEAS
Casuariiformes, CASSOWARIES, EMUS
Apterygiformes, KIWIS
Tinamiformes, TINAMOUS
Sphenisciformes, PENGUINS
Gaviiformes, LOONS
Podicipediformes, GREBES
Procellariiformes, PETRELS, ALBATROSSES, SHEARWATERS, FULMARS
Pelecaniformes, PELICANS, GANNETS, BOOBIES, CORMORANTS, SHAGS, DARTERS, FRIGATE BIRDS
Ciconiiformes, HERONS, BITTERNS, FLAMINGOS, IBISES, SPOONBILLS, STORKS
Anseriformes, DUCKS, GEESE, SWANS,

SCREAMERS
Falconiformes, FALCONS, VULTURES, KITES, EAGLES, BUZZARDS, HAWKS, KESTRELS, OSPREYS, SECRETARY BIRDS
Galliformes, TURKEYS, PHEASANTS, PARTRIDGES, GROUSE, PEAFOWL
Gruiformes, CRANES, RAILS, COOTS, BUSTARDS
Charadriiformes, JACANAS, OYSTERCATCHERS, AVOCETS, COURSERS, PLOVERS, LAPWINGS, SNIPE, SKUAS, GULLS, TERNS, SKIMMERS, AUKS
Pteroclidiformes, SAND GROUSE
Columbiformes, DOVES, PIGEONS
Psittaciformes, PARROTS, PARAKEETS, LORIES, LORIKEETS, COCKATOOS, MACAWS
Cuculiformes, CUCKOOS, TURACOS, HOATZIN
Strigiformes, OWLS

Caprimulgiformes, NIGHTJARS, NIGHTHAWKS, FROGMOUTHS, OILBIRDS, POTOOS
Apodiformes, SWIFTS, HUMMINGBIRDS
Coliiformes, MOUSEBIRDS
Trogoniformes, TROGONS
Coraciiformes, KINGFISHERS, TODIES, MOTMOTS, BEE EATERS, ROLLERS, HOOPOES, HORNBILLS
Piciformes, WOODPECKERS, BARBETS, JACAMARS, PUFFBIRDS, HONEY GUIDES, TOUCANS
Passeriformes, PERCHING BIRDS (e.g., larks, swallows, shrikes, wrens, thrushes, warblers, sunbirds, honey eaters, buntings, blackbirds, finches, weavers, sparrows, starlings, birds of paradise, crows)

Glossary

adaptation A body part or behavior that helps an organism survive in its environment.

camouflage The colors, shapes, or structures that enable an organism to blend with its surroundings.

cells Microscopic units that are the building blocks of all living things.

chlorophyll A green chemical in plant and algae cells that is needed for making food, in the process called photosynthesis.

courtship Finding and attracting a mate.

cytoplasm Material between the cell membrane and the nucleus.

digestion The mechanical and chemical breakdown of food into substances the body can use for growth and energy.

egg The female reproductive cell that is fertilized by a male sperm cell.

embryo An early stage in the development of organisms that are produced by sexual reproduction.

environment The surroundings of an organism or organisms.

evolution Change in organisms over a long period of time.

excretion The removal from the body of wastes that are created during metabolism.

extinct No longer in existence.

fertilization The union of sperm and egg, which leads to the development of a new organism.

food chain The order in which a series of organisms feeds on one another in an ecosystem.

food web A system of overlapping and interconnecting food chains.

fossils Remains or traces of living things that have been preserved in rocks, ice, and other materials.

genes Structures in the nucleus of cells that determine the traits of organisms.

germination The growth, or sprouting, of a spore or seed.

habitat The environment in which an organism has its home.

heredity The physical characteristics that are passed on to an individual by its parents; heredity is controlled by genes.

hibernation A seasonal period of rest when the body processes slow down.

metabolism The chemical processes in cells that are essential to life.

migration The seasonal movement of animals.

organism A living thing.

photosynthesis The chemical process by which green plants and algae make food.

plankton Microscopic and near-microscopic organisms that float in water.

pollen A tiny grain produced by the male part of most plants; it contains a sperm cell.

pollination The transfer of pollen from the male part to the female part of most plants; a necessary step if fertilization is to take place in these plants.

predator An animal that kills other animals for food.

prey Animals that are eaten by other animals.

reproduction The process by which organisms create other members of their species.

respiration The exchange of gases between an organism and its environment; the use of oxygen by the cells.

species A group of organisms that share more traits with one another than with other organisms and that can reproduce with one another.

sperm The male reproductive cell that fertilizes a female egg.

stimulus A change in the environment that is detected by an organism.

venom Poison.

For Further Reading

Ardley, Neil. *Science Book of the Senses*. San Diego, CA: Harcourt Brace Jovanovich Juvenile Books, 1992.

Behme, Robert L. *Incredible Plants: Oddities, Curiosities & Eccentricities*. New York: Sterling, 1992.

Clarke, Barry. *Amphibian*. New York: Alfred A. Knopf, 1993.

Julivert, Maria A. *Fascinating World of Spiders*. Hauppauge, NY: Barron, 1992.

Landau, Elaine. *Interesting Invertebrates: A Look at Some Animals Without Backbones*. New York: Franklin Watts, 1991.

Losito, Linda. *Birds: The Plant-and Seed-Eaters*. New York: Fact On File, 1989.

Madgwick, Wendy. *Fungi & Lichens*. Madison, NJ: Raintree Steck-Vaughn, 1990.

Matthews, Rupert. *The Age of Mammals*. New York: Franklin Watts, 1990.

McCarthy, Colin, and Arnold, Nick. *Reptile*. New York: Alfred A. Knopf, 1991.

Nardo, Don. *Germs: Mysterious Microorganisms*. San Diego, CA: Lucent Books, 1991.

Parker, Steve. *Fish* (Eyewitness Books). New York: Alfred A. Knopf, 1990.

Sabin, Francene. *Ecosystems and Food Chains*. Mahwah, NJ: Troll Associates, 1985.

Snodgrass, M.E. *Environmental Awareness: Water Pollution*. Marco, FL: Bancroft-Sage, 1991.

Stidworthy, John. *Insects*. New York: Franklin Watts, 1989.

Tesar, Jenny. *Endangered Habitats*. New York: Facts On File, 1991.

Index